DEAR CATHY & CLAIRE

This is a Prion book

First published in Great Britain in 2006 by Prion
An imprint of the Carlton Publishing Group
20 Mortimer Street
London W1T 3JW

Jackie is a trade mark of and © DC Thomson &
Co Ltd 2006. All feature material, illustrations and
photographs © DC Thomson & Co Ltd 2006.

13-digit ISBN: 1-85375-603-2
10-digit ISBN: 978-1-85375-603-0

Edited and compiled by Lorna Russell

Senior Art Editor: Emma Wicks
Design: Anita Ruddell
Production: Caroline Alberti

PRINTED IN SINGAPORE

Jackie

DEAR CATHY & CLAIRE

The best of your favourite problem page

Contents

Foreword by Kerry MacKenzie
(Cathy & Claire 1971-1972)

Foreword

I felt I was the luckiest person in the world when, fresh from Aberdeen University in 1971, not only did I land a job on Britain's trendiest teen mag – but the job was Cathy & Claire! Heck, it seemed only yesterday that I'd been a faithful *Jackie* reader myself – as the oldest of four sisters, I'd had to fight on a weekly basis for first dibs on it. And when it was finally mine, the first page I turned to, in common with every other girl in my class, was Cathy & Claire! I'd even sent the wise "pair" the odd angst-ridden letter!

On hearing about my fab new job, the response of my more cynical pals was along the lines of, well, that'll be a doddle – no one ever writes to problem pages, so all you'll have to do is make up a few letters once a week.

Boy, were they wrong, wrong, wrong! (Well, I knew that.)

Every day, around 100 letters arrived for Cathy & Claire and it was my job to answer them. Luckily, it soon became apparent that a sizeable proportion revolved around the same couple of dozen topics, so to save time, not to mention my sanity, I created a series of standard responses.

Most of the problems broadly reflected the content of the magazine – *Jackie* was about romance and fun, not sex and drugs. Not surprisingly, by far the most frequent question was "I really fancy this boy – how can I get him to notice me?"

to which the Cathy & Claire stock reply included the simple but oh-so-effective line – and I have to credit this to the talented and much-missed journalist Les Daly who also debuted on *Jackie* – "Just keep smiling and saying hello!"

It struck me over the years how timeless this beautifully simple advice was for the romantically inclined – every bit as accurate a barometer of a bloke's interest today as it was in the 70s. And useful no matter what your age or circumstances – works just as well for the divorce-bruised-but-unbeaten 50-year-old as the still sweetly innocent pre-teen who's just begun to notice there's something oddly interesting about those strange creatures called boys.

Now, in these strife-torn times, it occurs to me it wouldn't be a bad idea for world leaders to adopt some of that C & C ethos. Seems to me it would be that much harder to engage in war when you keep the lines of communication open with a smile on your face.

My time as Cathy & Claire still ranks as one of the most satisfying jobs I had. I'm figuring that if you're holding this book in your hands, you're just as avid an ex-Cathy & Claire fan as I am. I hope you get as much enjoyment from the following pages as I did.

Have fun – and don't forget to keep smiling and saying hello!

Kerry MacKenzie (*Cathy & Claire 1971-1972*)

Do You Actually Open Our Letters?

DEAR CATHY & CLAIRE—After reading Jackie for some time, now, I've come to the conclusion that you don't bother opening your letters but just make up the problems and stick your advice on the end. I've written to you loads of times and never had a letter published.

Well, luv, we've opened this one, haven't we?

Every letter, and boy, do we get 'em, is opened and read. We pick problems which, we feel, will help the majority, as we get a rough idea of what bothers most of you in the letters.

Those with stamped addressed envelopes are answered separately.

If you think about it, it's far easier for us to open letters and read them, problems provided, than sit racking our brains for imaginary situations.

We haven't got the time, luv, and the volume of mail provides us with plenty of scope.

Perhaps your problems weren't suited to the page, in which case, if you'd enclosed a s.a.e. we'd have given our advice privately.

We can't force you to believe us, but we'd hate you to think we treated your worries lightly!

How Can We Get Them To The Dry Cleaners?

DEAR CATHY & CLAIRE — My friend and I have a rather unusual problem.

You see we're going out with two boys and wherever we go they always wear the same suits. We know new clothes are expensive, but theirs are getting really dirty, and they just won't have them cleaned.

We've tried to drop hints but they don't seem to catch on. Please help — both them and us!

Well, hinting's all very well, but it doesn't work in this case, does it! We're afraid you'll have to be a bit more obvious about it — i.e. TELL THEM! It's a case for straight talking, this is; and you *can* do it without being rude.

If you're going out with a bloke, after all, you should feel close enough to him to be able to say more or less what you like, within reason, and it sounds reasonable enough to us to have a quiet word about nasty clothes!

So just point out that they are tatty, or grubby, or whatever, and that you'd just prefer it if they put on something a bit more presentable, please! No point in hinting and feeling aggrieved and writing to us about it. Give it straight to them.

Of course, just telling them might not make any difference. They may *like* going around like rag-bags and may resent anyone trying to change them. But if you really feel that strongly about it, then you'll just have to take the risk and tell them. Good luck!

A Botched Job

DEAR CATHY & CLAIRE — My friend makes lots of her own clothes, and when I asked her to make a dress for me, she agreed. I spent about three pounds on the material because it was for a special occasion, and counting the cost of the zip and dress pattern the whole thing came to about four pounds.

She went shopping with me and we bought a lovely pale pink needlecord material — she said there would be no problem, although she hadn't attempted the pattern before.

Well, she made an absolute mess of it. She cut it the wrong way, and to salvage what was left of the material, she had to make it into a short pinafore instead of a full-length dress. Even then, it didn't sit properly at the shoulders, and I could barely hide my disappointment.

She's offered to pay for the material, but I don't want her to do that.

This has upset our friendship, and I don't know what to do to put things right again. I just wish I'd never thought of it.

You have our sympathy, love. This really has put you into a bad situation, none of which has really been your fault.

If you feel you cannot accept full compensation for the material, why not suggest that she gives you half of the total amount? It won't really be enough to get you a new dress, but it will salve her conscience and make her feel slightly better.

Bring the whole thing out into the open and agree to forget about it. Harping on about past mistakes will only aggravate the situation, and perhaps lose you a friend.

Try to keep in mind that she meant well, no matter what.

And next time you want a dress made, go to a professional. It'll cost a bit more, but you can be sure of good results!

They're Calling My Sister Names

DEAR CATHY & CLAIRE — My older sister is unmarried and has recently had a baby boy. Our family were naturally shocked at first but we've got over it and accepted the situation. Our friends and neighbours were great too, and now we all dote on little Jason.

My trouble is the girls in my class at school. As I live in a small town, they've all found out about my sister and they've started to be really rotten to me. They shout terrible names about my sister and it's beginning to get me down.

I don't want to tell my mum as I think she'd get really upset. I've already had a shouting match with one of the girls and I'm sure I'll end up with no friends if this goes on much longer. Is there anything I can do about this?

Although this is very difficult for you, the best thing you can possibly do is to ignore these girls' remarks and show them that you will not be upset or riled by their teasing. We've no doubt that they'll get tired of their game in time.

Show them that you're not ashamed of your family. Take the baby out for walks in the pram, if your sister lets you. Even although these girls are being hard and cruel just now, we'll bet they melt a bit at the sight of a little baby. Most girls do.

If they don't though, don't worry about it. After all; you don't *really* want to be friends with such stupid, insensitive people, anyway, do you . . .?

13

Am I Normal?

DEAR CATHY & CLAIRE — Do all girls feel inclined to write romantic poems?

I'm a romantic type of person, and though I often feel like writing poetry I also think it's silly for me to do this. Do you think it's just immaturity?

Well, if the urge to write poetry and actually doing so were immature and silly, there wouldn't be too much of it published, would there?

We don't know if *everybody* wants to, but we think it's great if you're one of those who does! It's fantastic that you've got enough feeling and sensitivity to want to express it, and creating anything yourself can give you a tremendous amount of satisfaction.

We're not saying you're going to burst into print, but next time you feel like writing anything don't sit around wondering if you *ought* to feel that way, just get out that pen and start scribbling — even if it'll please no-one but yourself!

Is This The Road To Debt?

DEAR CATHY & CLAIRE — What is your honest opinion of mail-order catalogues? I've just started work, and one of the girls brought one in, and there are some fabulous boots in there that I could afford nicely if I paid weekly. But when I mentioned it to my mother, she got mad, and said I'd get myself into debt before I knew it.

Honestly, though, if I have to save to get the ready cash to buy the boots, it will take ages. My wages aren't that much, and it seems stupid not to take the opportunity.

Well, we think mail-order catalogues are a very good way of buying things, providing you don't go absolutely mad and order loads of things, so that your weekly payments are way above what you can afford. That's just plain silly, and this is probably what your mother is afraid of. She's no doubt thinking your wages are going to your head a little but we agree, boots are a necessity for bad weather.

As long as you buy them, and clear the bill before starting on anything else, you won't get out of your depth.

Assure your mother, too, that in a reputable club, the prices are the same as shop prices, as far as branded goods go, and comparable with the shops in fashion goods.

They're Being Nasty About Her Behind Her Back

DEAR CATHY & CLAIRE — My friend is a really nice person, but she is always in a rush and consequently looks very untidy. Her clothes are often un-ironed, her shoes are rarely polished and her hair looks as though it's hardly seen a comb.

I'm not being nasty, but I heard a couple of girls talking about her the other day and I was really upset about it.

I've never bothered about her untidy ways before, but I feel that I should try to help her before she overhears someone as I'm sure she'd be very upset if she did.

How can I help without offending her?

Well, it is an awfully difficult problem, but we think that you should try to change her gradually. For instance, when you arrange to go out, you could collect her at her home, but make sure that you arrive too early so that you can offer her a hand; you could try saying something such as " I'll polish your shoes while you iron your dress, if you like."

We doubt whether she's really lazy, love, probably just absent-minded, so maybe your offer will jolt her memory.

It's a shame when someone is really a very nice person but everyone gets the wrong impression about them, so try to make her take more pride in her appearance.

My Sister's Boyfriend Is Cheating With Me

DEAR CATHY AND CLAIRE — For months now, I've been feeling terribly guilty. I know what I should do, but I just can't!

You see, it's my sister's boyfriend, Brian. She thinks they're getting engaged soon, but for the past five months he's been seeing me behind her back. He says he loves me, really, but hasn't the heart to finish with Sally, my sister.

I know I should tell him to get lost, but I like him better than any other boy I've been out with.

I thought about telling Sally but that would be sure to cause a terrible scene and I want to avoid that.

You want to avoid Brian, too, if you've any sense at all! How can you possibly believe what he tells you? He's allowed this terrible situation to drift on for five whole months. How your sister has remained unaware of what's going on simply amazes us!

It's Sally we feel sorry for — she has a lying two-timing boyfriend and a sister who has been deceiving her all this time.

You've got a choice, love, you must stop seeing Brian now and either tell him to be honest with Sally and apologise, or you'll have to risk hurting Sally and tell her yourself.

You may fall out with Sally for a short time, but as least you'll have the satisfaction of knowing that you're both well rid of a boy who certainly isn't worth fighting for!

19

He's Trying To Take Advantage Of Me

DEAR CATHY AND CLAIRE — You've just got to help me. Every Friday night, I go round to my friend's house to play records and have a talk. However, every time she leaves the room now, her father sits beside me and tries to kiss me. My friend's mum died three years ago, but I don't think this is any excuse for his behaviour, do you? He always makes me feel welcome in the house, but, although I don't want to appear rude, I sometimes feel like swearing at him. My friend doesn't know anything about it. Tell me what to do. I'm 16.

Probably a sharp warning from you will put him in his place. If you let him get away with it, he'll take that as encouragement, so do something.

"Act your age." "My boyfriend won't be pleased to hear about this and neither will my parents." Or a sharp dig in the ribs should give him the hint that his advances aren't welcome.

All he probably wants to do is prove to himself that he still appeals to young girls. Disillusion him!

I Hate My New Haircut

DEAR CATHY & CLAIRE — I'm writing to you as a last resort — you see, mine's not that much of a problem, but it's worrying me terribly.

I've got a Saturday job in a hairdresser's and I get along really well with all the girls there. Since the style had grown out of my hair, I asked one of the girls to cut it. Well, she really made a mess of it. It's hacked about and is quite short now and I can't do a thing with it. I feel very self-conscious about it, but I don't want to upset her by going and having it re-done somewhere else. And of course, I daren't tell her I don't like it. Please tell me what to do!

It's not the end of the world you know — there are lots of ways out! First and foremost, hair grows! It's amazing the difference you'll see in only a few weeks — even a very short style will look miles softer and you'll have got used to it, too! So there's no need to go rushing out to do something about it immediately, especially if you don't want to make it too obvious you detest the new style. And there's no guarantee that any other hairdresser can make it look exactly the way you want it, now, anyway.

Then instead of having this girl re-style it, just tell her very firmly that you've decided you want to grow it. And make sure she doesn't get her hands on it again!

If and when you do want something else done with it, there are all sorts of excuses you can make, like there's this cousin of yours who's dying to cut it for you, or it'll have to be done during the week for this special party you're going to, or you know someone who had their hair done exactly as you want it so you're going to the same hairdresser.

You see? It's not worth wasting time worrying over that one!

I Dread His Kisses

DEAR CATHY & CLAIRE — I have the most ridiculous problem with my boyfriend, Dave, and I know lots of other girls have come across this at some time or another, so please print it and help us out!

My boyfriend and I have been going out with each other for a long time and we're both very fond of each other. The trouble is, I've never really liked him kissing me.

This sounds horrid and picky, I know, but really it's reached the point where I dread being alone with him in case he kisses me.

I've tried subtle hints, but they don't work. I don't want to hurt his feelings and I don't want to lose him, but I just can't go on like this any more! Please, what can I do?

From what you've said, it doesn't sound as if he's a boy you really want to get serious about!

You may be very fond of him, but you could just want a friendship with him, not a special boyfriend/girlfriend relationship. You obviously can't tell him outright that you want to carry on going out with him but you don't want him to get near you, so why don't you just change the whole relationship? Then you can go out, meet other people, and when there's someone you *do* want to kiss you, you'll know it's time to get serious about them.

And strangely enough, going out with Dave on a purely friendly basis may help your problem in other ways. By removing the feeling that you think you *have* to kiss him because he's your *boyfriend*, you'll be able to build up a much more natural relationship and you may find that kissing him will come naturally! Which is how things should be, after all!

She Had Her Eye On Him All Along

DEAR CATHY & CLAIRE — I broke up with my boyfriend two weeks ago. I'd been a bit fed up with the way he was treating me. He was always late in meeting me, never phoned me and was sometimes a bit off hand with me. But I wouldn't have chucked him, if it hadn't been for this other girl at work.

She was really sympathetic and consoled me when I was upset about him. She told me that he was no good, that a decent boy wouldn't treat a girl in that way, and she egged me on to make the break with him.

So I did — and now she's going out with him! I don't know whether I'm angry or upset. I'd like to get my own back, though.

We don't really think that anyone can talk someone into finishing with a boy they're really keen on. You must have had your doubts about him yourself. So you can't really put all the blame for the finished romance on this girl.

However, she certainly wouldn't make a good friend, if she's as two-faced as she appears. You can gain some consolation from the fact that neither he nor she are particularly desirable as a boy friend or a best friend. Tell yourself that they deserve each other!

Put the whole miserable episode behind you, and don't let yourself get jealous or bitter about them. They're just not worth it. What you need now are a few sincere girl friends and considerate boyfriends. So don't waste time plotting revenge — get out and meet new people.

I Have Nobody To Go Around With

DEAR CATHY & CLAIRE — My problem is I've got no real friends.

When I started secondary school two years ago I kept to one friend, Yvonne, but then she started going around with another girl, and I fell out with her about that. I do speak to people at school but I don't go around with them.

There's this girl, Christine, who I was sitting next to last year and she says I can go around with her, but I don't know if I should. I'm really mixed up. Please help!

Don't get mixed up, believe us; it's clear as a bell—if Yvonne can't be trusted to stay loyal to you, you really can't be expected to wait around for her! She's gone away from you, and there's absolutely no reason why you shouldn't make other friends.

Whether your special friend should be Christine, is really up to you. She's offered you her friendship and we think if there's any doubt in your mind about whether you like her enough to be close and loyal to her, you should leave things cool and stay at a distance from her. But it sounds to us as though it's a friendship worth going after, especially as you've been sitting together and must have some things in common.

But remember, friendship's basically a matter of liking people and giving to them — stop thinking of it as a mad scramble for "someone to go around with", and you'll find you start getting those "real" friends you're after!

I'm The Odd One Out

DEAR CATHY & CLAIRE — Most of the girls in my class at school are continually discussing what they are doing at weekends, who they are going out with and so on. It's a tragedy if they even have to stay in the house for one evening.

I'm not at all like them. I'm perfectly happy to stay in with a good book. It isn't that I never go out, but is there something wrong with me because I'm not more sociable?

No, love, there isn't. You're one of those fortunate people who are independent enough to be happy without relying on other people to entertain you. This is fine, but the danger is that you could cut yourself off a bit from the rest of the world.

There may come a time when you feel you've been missing out on these weekend outings and you'd like a boyfriend of your own, so try to keep in touch with your school friends and perhaps go out with them sometimes. You may even find that you enjoy yourself.

After all, it isn't really fair to say that you don't like something without giving it a try.

Don't Tell Me It's Just A Crush!

DEAR CATHY & CLAIRE — You've probably heard this a hundred times before but I'm absolutely crazy about David Cassidy. I've felt like this for ages, and, please believe me, it's NOT just a childish crush. I've reached the stage where I just can't sleep at night for thinking about him and now even my school work is suffering.

I'm not ugly and loads of boys have asked me out, but I'm just not interested.

Please help me, how can I meet David?

We do receive hundreds of letters just like yours, love, and we understand how you feel. But what you feel *is* a crush — honestly! Your emotion can't be described as love because it's impossible to love someone you don't actually know. What you DO know is his image projected by his publicists, and it's this dream you've fallen for.

We've all had these sort of dreams at some time or another and they're lovely, we agree! But what you mustn't do is allow these dreams to take over from reality and spoil your chances of having a good relationship with a boy who IS attainable.

We're sorry we can't help you to meet David, but have you thought about what you'd do if you *did* actually come face to face with him? Nothing more would come of the meeting and it would only be an anticlimax to your dream wouldn't it?

By all means, think of David, but at the same time go out and mix with your friends and have a good time. Once you have a boyfriend of your own these dreams really will fade.

Please give it a try — we're sure you'll find we're right.

His Hair Style Is Ruining Our Relationship

DEAR CATHY & CLAIRE, I'm really miserable. I've been going with my boyfriend for three months — and he's the trouble.

You see, it's his hair. MY hair is shoulder length, but his is a good five inches longer than mine — honestly!

I love him a lot, I'm sure I do. He's a fantastic boy and he's good to me in almost everything. But if we go to the pictures, usherettes laugh and snigger at him. If we go for a walk, there are always kids hanging round and laughing at us.

My parents get upset with me and they tell me that all our neighbours talk about me. My boy tells me he loves me, but if he did, surely he would get his hair cut, when it's making life so miserable!

Should I finish with him?

Suppose the best way to get round this is to try finding out WHY he insists on wearing his hair so long.

No doubt the price of haircuts has SOMETHING to do with it — but there's more to it than that.

Could it be that he wants attention, that he wants people to notice him? If you think this is the case, then perhaps a little more affection from yours truly could make a difference.

Maybe he's just plain stubborn — the more you ask him to get it cut, the more determined he is to have it long.

Since we don't know your bloke, we really can't say. It's a case of finding out what's bothering him and trying to fix it . . . or putting up with it . . . or giving HIM up . . .

33

My Platforms Are Frightening Him Off

DEAR CATHY & CLAIRE — Although everyone always tells me that I suit being "petite," I'd love to be tall. Since platform shoes have been fashionable, I've been really happy as they add quite a few inches to my height.

The other week Steve, one of the boys at school, asked me out, and as I'd liked him for ages, I said yes. I knew that he wasn't very tall either, but this didn't bother me as he was a little bit bigger than me. I never thought about the fact that I'd only seen him when we were in school uniform and I was wearing very low-heeled shoes. When I met him outside the cinema, we both nearly died of horror, as I was about three inches taller than him!

I've been out with him a few times since then, but he always walks along a little distance away from me and never moves closer or holds my hand.

He's really nice and I wouldn't like to finish with him, but it seems to me that we're getting nowhere at the moment.

Steve must like you a lot, love, or he wouldn't keep asking you out. The reason that he walks apart from you when you're out is probably because he's self-conscious about the difference in your height.

If you really like him, then why don't you invest in a pair of lower shoes? Small, neat platforms are just as fashionable nowadays as large ones, if not more so. After all, it's in a good cause!

35

How Do We Get Them To Talk To Us?

DEAR CATHY & CLAIRE — My friend and I really fancy these two boys, but we don't know how to get to know them.

We often see them in town and they sometimes smile at us but they both seem to be pretty shy.

It's driving us mad as we just don't know how we can get to speak to them, let alone go out with them.

Apart from falling at their feet or grabbing them by the throats, how can we get to know them?

It looks like you'll have to give these boys some encouragement — maybe quite a lot, depending on how shy they are.

Take (or make!) any opportunity you can to talk to them. If possible, arrange to bump into them accidentally when you know they're going to be somewhere. Get talking to them about anything and everything — they'll soon get the message.

There's no need to ask them out — that could scare them off and spoil all your carefully laid plans. Just show you like them, and if they want to ask you out, they will do — even if it takes a bit of time for them to pluck up courage.

Be patient, and we'll keep our fingers crossed for you!

How Can I Stop Her Copying?

DEAR CATHY & CLAIRE — I've got a problem I really don't know how to cope with. It's my friend Pam. She's not very clever but she really needs to get her 'O' levels so she can go to college to do window dressing. She's great at art but pretty bad at everything else.

Well, the trouble is that she sits beside me in class, and honestly, she copies every bit of work I do.

I've told her she should try to do her own work, but all she says is that I should know that she can't and I should know how important it is to her.

I really think it's wrong, but how can I tell her? I'm sure she won't talk to me if I don't let her copy.

We're afraid some straight talking is the answer here. You've got to tell Pam that, however much she wants to go to college, she *must* work on her own.

Point out to her that she'll never learn *anything* from copying from you and that you are really hindering her more than helping her. Suggest to her that she has a talk with her teacher about her work. After all, this is the person who's in the best position to help.

You've got to think of your own safety, too. You'll be found out sooner or later by your teacher, you know, and then you'll *both* be called cheats.

Pam's really taking the easy way out, you know — and she's not being very fair to you.

So tell her all this quietly and calmly, and we really don't think she'll stop speaking to you. If she does, though, well, all we can say is that she's not really a very worthwhile friend, is she?

I Wish He'd Just Be Himself

DEAR CATHY & CLAIRE — My boyfriend is absolutely obsessed with films and T.V. programmes.

After he's been watching a western, he develops a Texas drawl and a John Wayne swagger, and after a James Bond film, he acts very cool and man-of-the-worldish.

It's most embarrassing when we're with a crowd as all of our friends laugh at him. How can I cure him?

Before you try to cure him, try to decide whether he's just putting on this act to amuse himself and everyone else, or whether he's just being immature and silly.

It seems to us that since he doesn't mind being laughed at, it's probably the former reason — if so, why spoil everyone's fun?

If you feel that he's just acting very immaturely, then have a good straight talk with him and let him know how you feel. On the other hand you might not be as keen on him as you think you are if his behaviour embarrasses you so much. Think about it.

In the meantime we'd avoid going to see any Dracula films!

41

I'm Nearly A Foot Taller Than My Best Friend

DEAR CATHY & CLAIRE — Please don't laugh! My problem is really depressing me. You see, because I'm nearly five feet ten I've always found it difficult to mix with people my own age.

As if this isn't bad enough my friend has the opposite problem. She's tiny. Barely five feet, I think, and we really do look like freaks.

The trouble is I'm gangly. At least she looks petite and I'm sure she'd have lots of boyfriends if it wasn't for me. I really dwarf her.

We get on so well it would be a pity to split up, but for her sake I often wonder if it would be better for her to go and find another friend nearer to her size.

I've lost hope already. What should I do? We're fifteen, by the way.

She probably feels the same way, love. Looking up at you she probably thinks to herself that it must be great to stand out in a crowd and to be able to do all the things tall people can do that short ones can't.

If she wasn't happy with the way things were she'd find someone else, we're sure, but she likes you for yourself. As you said you get on really well and that's what counts.

Confidence is what counts and loads of personality. Show everyone what nice people you are and forget about your size.

We've said it before and we'll say it again. Some day some boy is going to find your height your most attractive feature. The same goes for your friend. It would be such a boring world if we were all the same — and we admire your individuality!

I've Fallen For A Married Man

DEAR CATHY AND CLAIRE — The other evening, a colleague of dad's came to dinner and I think I'm in love with him. He's in his early thirties and married, but very attractive. He was nice to me, said I had pretty eyes and said I'd have to go to his house to return the visit. I'm sixteen and old enough to know my own mind, but I don't want to break up his marriage as he has a young son.

If you're sixteen, you're old enough to know better! This friend of your dad's was only being polite to his host's daughter. The invitation was probably meant to mean that you were included in the visit for your mum and dad.

It's quite natural for you to fancy an older man — if it wasn't him, perhaps it would be a teacher at school. Accept all compliments gracefully, but save the flirting for lads nearer your own age.

I'm Too Scared To Go On A Date

DEAR CATHY & CLAIRE — A boy in my class at school has asked me to go out with him and I'd like to but I'm scared. What am I supposed to do and say when I'm out with him? I've worried so much about this, I don't think I could go out with him, but then I'm too shy to tell him to his face that I don't want to go.

Please help.

Stop getting into a panic! Take a deep breath and relax. Now you are ready to think this over sensibly.

We think you *should* go out with this boy. Because let's face it, if you run away now, you could go on running for a very long time and it's hard to face up to something once you've been running away for a long time. So come on, say "yes, you'd love to go out with him", and that's half the battle won.

Really though, you shouldn't be thinking of it as a struggle. When it comes to going out together, if you bear in mind he may be as nervous as you are, you can concentrate on helping him to relax. That way, you'll forget your own shyness and before the evening's over you'll find you're actually enjoying yourself.

Does He Like Me Or My Friend?

DEAR CATHY & CLAIRE — My friend and I both fancy the same boy. He's at our school and he's really nice looking. Recently he's started coming about with my friend and me and this makes things very awkward. Because we both fancy him we've become very competitive. I know I can't help it but this bitchiness is spoiling our friendship.

I don't know what to do about this as I don't want to lose him. I hope he fancies me, but how can I tell?

What can I do to settle this before our friendship is ruined?

First of all, are you really sure that this boy fancies one of you? He could just enjoy your company, and if this is the case, you'll both have to accept him as a friend.

If he does fancy one of you he'll make a move — but if you don't know, then *we* certainly can't predict the outcome!

So you'll just have to wait and see. Whatever happens, don't let the situation ruin your friendship. It's not worth it.

If he does fancy one of you — the other will have to accept the situation gracefully.

We hope things work out the way you want them to!

My Glasses Get In The Way

DEAR CATHY & CLAIRE — I wear glasses and that in itself isn't a problem, as I don't think they look too bad on me, it's just that I don't know what to do with them when a boy asks me to dance.

If I don't wear them, I can't see a thing, but if I keep them on while I dance, they dig into the boy, so I'm not relaxed because I'm trying to avoid him all the time. Do you think I ought to hold them in my hand while I dance, or will that look stupid?

Please help, and don't suggest I buy contact lenses because I'm 14 and couldn't possibly afford them.

This needs a leetle bit of cunning and female ingenuity. You realise specs suit you, so play them up to their best advantage. So they dig into him a bit — make a joke of it! A boy appreciates a girl who can laugh at herself, and anyway, if you get that close to him, they can't be such a disadvantage, can they? And surely a little thing like a nudge from your specs isn't going to put him off if he's really keen?

Explain to him before you start dancing that you'd take 'em off but he'd probably end up with 10 cracked toes if you do — we're pretty sure he'll see the sense in that!

I Have A Lazy Mum

DEAR CATHY & CLAIRE — Since a few weeks ago my mum has started giving me £1 a week. With this I'm expected to buy my own clothes and shoes, tights and all other accessories.

I'm only 13 and I have to do all my own washing and ironing. Even on school days my mum doesn't get up until 8.30, so I have to get my own breakfast and I'm always late for school. My dad never stops moaning and the house is always untidy.

Sometimes my mum pretends she's ill and stays in bed hoping I'll do the housework. I get so unhappy, once I even ran away and spent the night at a friend's, then when I got back the following evening my mum wasn't even pleased to see me. Please can you help me.

It does sound stiff that you're virtually having to look after yourself at home, and though we can't presume to guess at your mother's motives, housework and meals should be her responsibility.

So the most positive step you can take at the moment is to talk to another adult; try someone else in your family, or if there's no-one you find sympathetic maybe a friend's mother or a teacher at school. After all, if the situation's making you miserable and restricted, it's got to be talked out and it could be that someone older than you will be able to get through to your mum on your behalf.

Maybe your mum's got problems, too, though, if she's shirking her responsibilities towards you and your dad like this? We don't know the situation in detail, only what you've written to us, so do get hold of someone you can spill it out to and who can examine it properly. We reckon you really need someone who's close to it to deal with it.

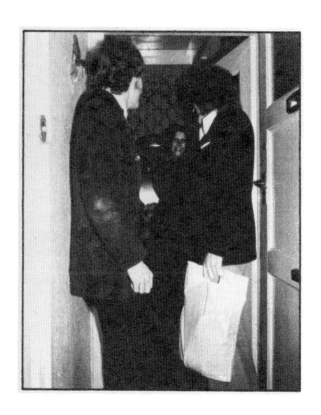

My Party Will Be Out Of Control

DEAR CATHY & CLAIRE — My parents are going away on holiday in two weeks' time. This is the first time I've been allowed to stay at home myself and I'm really looking forward to it.

I've told all my friends about this and we're all having a great time planning a party! Naturally I don't want my parents to find out so we've got to keep things quiet. Unfortunately, word has got around and now nearly everyone knows about it — including a rather wild crowd that lives fairly near here.

I'm beginning to get a bit worried now, but I must have this party — everyone will be mad if I don't. Please give me some advice because I don't know what to do. My parents would be mad if they found out.

Well, we're sorry to put a damper on your plans, but you really can't have this party. You know that yourself, don't you?

Your parents would be very hurt and angry if they found out about your plans — and quite rightly, too. After all, they're trusting you to stay at home on your own so you must act in a responsible way. Parties never turn out very well when you're feeling guilty and worried and it's very likely that some mark of the party would be left as evidence. It might only be a cigarette burn or two, but it could be much worse . . .

And think, your neighbours are going to know you're on your own and they're likely to be keeping an eye on you. They would definitely hear or see the party — and that's when the trouble will start . . .

We think you know the trouble this party could land you in, so please change your mind before it's too late. Of course it'll be difficult to tell your friends, but it has to be done. Ignore any criticism and don't let anyone change your mind.

And to cheer you and your friends up, why don't you plan a party when your parents are there and with their permission? This would be much, much safer!

When Will
He Kiss Me?

DEAR CATHY & CLAIRE — I'm 14 and I've been going out with my boyfriend for 6 weeks. The trouble is he hasn't kissed me yet. Where do you think I'm going wrong?

We can't imagine! But there's a sure way to find out. And it's this: next time you're out with your boyfriend, why not fling your arms round his neck and see what he does? You could have a pleasant surprise!

Our Dishy Doctor Makes Me Swoon

DEAR CATHY & CLAIRE — I always thought that doctors were middle-aged and boring — until I met our new doctor.

I had a dose of flu a couple of months ago and our new doctor came out to visit me. Honestly, I just about fainted when I saw him! He's tall, blond and has the most piercing blue eyes I've ever seen — and as well as all that he has a lovely soft, deep voice. When he said that I was much better and that he wouldn't need to call again, I was so upset that mum thought I was having a relapse!

I've been to the surgery a couple of times with made-up complaints, but I can't go on making up illnesses indefinitely as he's sure to guess the truth. Apart from that, my mum's convinced that I'm becoming a hypochondriac!

It seems to us love, that you've probably just developed a king-sized crush on an older, more mature man. You'd be surprised how many girls fall for people in authority such as doctors and teachers. You're not really in love with him; just infatuated.

As soon as you meet a nice boy who you really like, you'll forget about your doctor. But in the meantime it isn't fair to take up the doctor's valuable time with fake illnesses.

I'm A Soft Touch

DEAR CATHY & CLAIRE — I recently started secondary school and I joined up with another four girls.

The trouble is, when I bring in sweets and chewing-gum they all ask me for them continuously. I can't refuse because I'd feel too selfish and this means I usually end up with only a few sweets to myself. I know I'm a coward and badly lack confidence, but please help! I do get on well with these girls and I don't want to break the friendship.

Stop bringing sweets in! That's the short answer to that one, isn't it? If you don't have any, you can't give them away, and you'll stop feeling mean/cowardly/aggrieved. Could be you'll get better skin and teeth, too, by the way!

Experience teaches you lessons, though — people do take advantage of generosity, don't they? We don't think you're that weak; after all, it'd be a bit silly to start arguing over a few sweets, and it's nice of you to hand them round. The decent thing to do, though, would be for the others to return the generosity and take it in turns to bring goodies for each other. And, if they can't realise that, just quietly drop the habit altogether!

I'm A Good-Looking Boy Who Can't Get Girls

DEAR CATHY & CLAIRE — I know you don't often get letters from boys, but I'm sure you could help me with my problem.

I don't seem to be able to keep a girlfriend for more than a couple of weeks. I'm 17, very good-looking and always wear trendy gear so my appearance can't be the reason.

Some of my mates who don't care how they look, have gorgeous girlfriends who are madly in love with them and I just can't understand it.

There's one girl that I know fancies me but she's not very pretty or trendy and I don't really think she's good enough for me. I'm sure my mates would laugh at me if I went out with her.

There's obviously nothing wrong with your looks — but there's definitely something wrong with your attitude!

You're so selfish and self-centred it's not true. What girl wants a boyfriend who's so busy looking in the mirror he doesn't have a spare moment for her? You should be glad that there's at least one girl who's so blind to your faults, she actually wants to go out with you. So wake up to the fact that you're not every girl's dream-boy, develop an interest in other people and maybe then you'll discover that a girlfriend is not so hard to come by as you imagine . . .

57

They Won't Believe We Are Serious

DEAR CATHY & CLAIRE — I'm really depressed because everyone —including my parents —are against me. I'm thirteen and want to get engaged to Steve, who's fifteen. We've been going together for three weeks and are really in love.

I am attractive, although Steve is nothing to look at, which makes me think that I love him for himself. My parents are being completely selfish about the matter and just will not see my point of view.

But come on, love! How can you possibly expect your parents to take you seriously when you're only thirteen and talking about getting engaged to a boy you've only known for three weeks?! An engagement is a promise to marry, you know, and it's obvious your parents realise this — even if you don't!

Anyone who thinks they *must* love their boyfriend for himself because *they're* attractive and he's " nothing to look at," isn't ready to go steady, never mind get engaged!

So stop being so silly. Go on going out with Steve, have fun, and listen to your parents. They *are* right, you know!

Why Hasn't He Called?

DEAR CATHY & CLAIRE — Two weeks ago at a party, I got off with the most amazing boy I've ever met. He was just gorgeous, and we had a really great time together. Then he promised to phone me some time during the week, so we could arrange to go out again.

But I've stayed in every night since then, just waiting and he hasn't phoned. It's not as if he's phoned during the day either, as my Gran is in all day, and she'd answer it, if it did ring.

I'm so fed up. Do you think he's lost my phone number? Or maybe something's happened to him and he hasn't been able to phone? What can I do? I'm so desperate to see him again, but I don't know his address or even his surname.

Sorry love, but this seems to be a case of the old, old story. If this boy had really been keen, he'd have contacted you by now. And there really is no way *you* can contact him, is there?

But don't despair, because this happens to most of us at one time or another. We all meet someone we think is extra special, but it comes to nothing, 'cos they don't really share the same interest in us.

It's a big blow to our pride at the time, but honestly, we all get over it. And it's much easier to forget, once you realise that this boy of your dreams isn't interested enough. After all, a one-sided love affair isn't what you're after, is it?

So try to see this, and make a determined effort to put him to the back of your mind. Do get out and about as much as possible, and you'll soon meet other boys, who'll be more considerate. OK?

Are Lovebites Dangerous?

DEAR CATHY & CLAIRE — I've been really worried since my friends told me that lovebites can cause diseases, like cancer of the neck. Is there any way I can prevent this happening to me as I'm too frightened and embarrassed to go to my doctor?

It's about time this, and all the other old wives' tales, were cleared up! Lovebites do not cause cancer, or any other diseases. They are no more than harmless bruises. But, like any other bruise, they can sometimes be painful to touch.

However, lovebites are unsightly and certainly don't enhance the beauty of a graceful neck! In addition, your parents are quite likely to object to them. They might regard this as a sign that you are behaving foolishly, and the outcome could be an argument, or worse, a ban on you going out with boys altogether.

So, even though lovebites don't cause disease, it's probably best on all counts to try to avoid them.

HOW CAN I GET HIM TO STOP?

DEAR CATHY AND CLAIRE — Jeffrey is nice-looking and usually quite affectionate, but on Friday and Saturday nights he does sometimes get in with some boys who like to drink a lot, and when he's had a couple of beers, he changes completely.

He becomes extremely rude and shouts vulgar things at me, orders me about and generally makes me look a fool.

I keep telling him I'll leave him if he goes on like this, and although he always apologises for his behaviour next time he sees me, come Friday he's in the pub again. Is there any way I can stop him acting like this, without him hating me for nagging?

Are you really as worried by Jeffrey's behaviour as you make out? Or have you got the idea that this is something you just have to put up with if you want to keep a boy friend? Because you don't, you know. Not all boys get nasty with drink, and Jeffrey can obviously manage without his beer most of the week.

But while you *are* putting up with it so meekly, why should he bother to change? You threaten to leave him, yet here you are still going steady with him. No wonder he doesn't take your threats seriously.

You hold the answer to this problem. Arrange to spend Friday and Saturday nights at the cinema or in a disco — preferably a non-licensed one. Tell Jeffrey at the start of the week that he makes you feel small when he gets drunk, and that if he does it again you'll walk out.

And if, despite your plans, you end up in the pub and he starts on you, don't wait till he's thoroughly upset you — don't even say anything to him. Just get up and walk out. If you're old enough to go out with boys, you're old enough to see yourself home. And do go straight home — don't lurk outside the pub to see if he's going to follow you.

All Jeffrey needs is to be shown you mean what you say. You might have to walk out on him two or three times before he really believes you — but if you really want him to change, you'll do it.

But if he persists in being rude, we suggest that you leave him to his beer and boring behaviour, and get yourself a new and more considerate boy friend.

62

We Can't Agree On David Essex

DEAR CATHY & CLAIRE — I've been going out with this boy for a couple of weeks now. I really like him a lot, but one thing stops me being blissfully happy. You see, he is a couple of years older than I am and his taste in music doesn't agree with mine.

I'm a Bay City Roller and David Essex fanatic, but he can't stand them and he insists that I listen to the music that he likes — Led Zeppelin for example. Recently I had an opportunity to go and see a David Essex concert. He said that if I went he wouldn't want to see me again, so I decided not to go.

Although I'm willing to listen to his music, he won't listen to mine! How can I make him see that he is ruining our relationship?

We think that your boyfriend is being very thoughtless and it would serve him right if he lost you. It sounds as if you're a considerate person and we think he's taking advantage of your good nature.

If you like him a lot you may not appreciate our advice, but we really think he's going too far. If you let him boss you about over this, we think you're likely to have trouble in the future over more important things. Try talking to him about it and see what he says. Don't let him wrap you round his little finger . . . it's not worth it.

Help Me To Choose Between Them

DEAR CATHY & CLAIRE — There are two boys around town who both seem to fancy me, and have asked me out a couple of times. Trouble is, I don't know which one I like best. I can't decide between them at all, and I'd be grateful if you'd help, as I don't want them to think I'm just using them.

Jimmy is older and quite sophisticated, I suppose — he's got a good job, flash car, money and he dresses smoothly. He takes me to dances and out for meals, so I'm never bored. Robin's different altogether — he's a student, and never has two pennies to rub together, so all we do is go for a quiet drink, with his mates, or else we stay in at his place. I really think I fancy him more, but I have better times when I go out with Jimmy.

How can I choose which to stay with? It's too much of a strain going out with both.

What you'd really like us to do is to decide for you, but we can't really do this — it must be your own decision.

We can only make a few suggestions on how you can best make up your mind.

We think it sounds as if you really care for Robin, as you can like him for himself, but with Jimmy, you like him because he can afford to take you to smart, expensive places.

You say that you don't want to use either of them. Well, if so far you've been going out with them both and they both know about it — you could be getting the best of both worlds.

But if you feel you really can't cope and you do want to finish with one of them, ask yourself what you really want. Do you want just to have a good time and be taken out? Or do you want a more sincere, serious relationship? By answering that you should find out what you want.

Take your time, though, and don't do anything without thinking first.

67

Meeting Boys
Will Ruin My Holiday

DEAR CATHY & CLAIRE — I'm going on holiday in a couple of weeks with five of my friends. We've had this trip arranged for ages and I was really looking forward to it until we were all talking last week.

Two of the girls seem to be really determined to go out with every Spaniard they meet and I'm a bit worried about this. I'm not very confident with boys, and I don't want to get involved with any wild schemes for picking up Spaniards. I'm sure my friends are just going there for this reason and I'm quite upset about it.

It's too late to back down now but I'm not looking forward to going — is there anything I can do?

Yes! You really shouldn't worry about this. You won't have to do what these two girls are doing!

Anyway, we're pretty sure they're exaggerating. They're just looking forward to having lots of holiday romances! We doubt very much that they really intend to 'pick up' every Spaniard.

So try not to get upset, and look forward to your holiday. We're sure you'll have a great time and maybe even have a holiday romance of your own!

Meeting No Boys Ruined Our Holiday

DEAR CATHY & CLAIRE — This year my friend and I went on holiday together expecting to have a great time, but when we got there we were horrified to discover that the place was overrun with girls and that there was hardly a boy in sight.

What we would like to know is — where do all the boys go in the summer? If you know of any male-infested holiday resorts for next year, we'll be your friends for life.

One theory has it that all the members of this rare species go into hibernation over the summer months and only come out when the football season starts.

We think a hunting trip would be your best bet next summer and if you by any chance manage to track down any of that rare and elusive species, do send us a telegram and we'll come and join you.

I Should Have Stayed At School

DEAR CATHY & CLAIRE — I left school two years ago to work in a factory. I wanted to have lots of clothes and money to go out. Well, now I'm really sorry. I've got four 'O' levels and I wish I'd stayed on at school.

I hate the factory and I want to leave but I've got quite a big problem. I live with my mum and dad and they're not very well-off. They need the money I give them from my pay.

When I told them I wanted to leave and go to college they just about hit the roof. Now I don't know what to do. I'm so fed-up. Can you help?

First of all we think you should try and find a job you'd be happier in. With four 'O' levels you should find it quite easy to get another job. Go to your local Youth Employment Office and ask what sort of jobs are available to someone with your qualifications.

As it's not suitable for you to go to college full-time why don't you find out about night-classes in your area? You could sit certificate examinations at these colleges while you are still earning — and that means you would still be able to pay for your keep at home.

We're sure your parents won't object to this and we're sure you'll be a lot happier, too.

What Have I Done Wrong?

DEAR CATHY & CLAIRE — A rather mousey girl at our school has been telling us for months about this fantastic boy she's been going out with. Honestly, she hasn't stopped going on about him!

Well, last week I saw her in town with him and he's really horrible — small and ugly with glasses. I couldn't stop laughing. After all she'd said about him!

The next Monday at school I told all my friends and they just looked disgusted and walked away. I thought that they'd think it was funny, too! Now they're not even talking to me. Why not?

You mean we have to tell you? Come on — just have a good think about what you've done. It could do you the world of good . . .

What If I Get Homesick?

DEAR CATHY & CLAIRE — I'm 14 and have been given the chance of going abroad this summer with the school for two weeks.

Please don't think I'm being stupid but I've never been away from home before and I'm sure I'll be really homesick.

I'm sure you'll think I'm just being silly, but do you think I should go on this trip?

Don't worry, we don't think your problem is silly at all and we're sure it will be solved quite easily.

A lot of people get homesick — it's a natural feeling, you know — and it's something you'll get over in time. These school trips are usually very good for helping people to get over homesickness as you're with your friends all the time and don't have the time to get lonely!

Have a talk with your parents and tell them you're a bit worried about going away. They'll reassure you and no doubt they'll write to you while you're abroad!

Going away *will* do you good. It's the start of independence, you know. So don't worry about it now, and when summer comes, just enjoy your holiday! Cos you will, you know. Believe us!

My Friends Don't Understand Me

DEAR CATHY & CLAIRE — I don't think it matters what sort of clothes you wear and what sort of music you like — but all my friends seem to think it does. They say I don't look right when I wear a long skirt and like different music from them. They all wear tartan, and talk about nothing else but the Bay City Rollers.

I don't want to be like this. I like being different and doing what I want to do. I don't want to be influenced by other people but sometimes I can't help it. I know I shouldn't take any notice of other people, but sometimes it's difficult.

Have you any suggestions on how I can just forget about what my friends do and say?

You're doing quite well as it is! Of course you've every right to dress the way you want and act the way you want! Don't let yourself be bothered by other people — you're an individual, after all.

In a way, these other girls are probably jealous of your individuality and independence — you don't need to follow fashions and trends to give you confidence. Your friends will eventually accept you and stop trying to change you — so don't worry about them. You're obviously happy the way you are, so just keep on being yourself!

I Don't Want To Show Him Up

DEAR CATHY AND CLAIRE — I've only been out with Les a few times but I like him a lot and now his mother's invited me to tea with them on Sunday.

I don't want to go, but I don't see how I can get out of it without appearing rude. I'm sure I'll spill my tea all over the table or say something stupid.

Do you think that I should offer to help with the dishes afterwards? I'm not really sure about this, and I'm certain I'll break some of her best china or something if I do.

Please help me as I'm worried in case I make a fool of myself and let Les down.

Try not to worry so much, it's supposed to be a pleasant outing, not an ordeal. If you sit and brood about it, you'll just become even more tense and worried and then you'll feel awkward and become even more likely to do something silly. Have you given a thought to how Les must be feeling — or even his mum for that matter? They're probably both just as nervous as you are, if not more so.

When you get ready to go to Les's house, make sure you wear something that you feel comfortable in so that you won't have to fidget about. And don't perch on the edge of the seat, sit back and make yourself comfortable — you'll find that you'll relax much more easily that way.

No doubt Les's mum will try to find out all about you, so try to chat to her. After all, she can't be that bad when she has a son as nice as Les, can she?

When tea's over, you could offer to help with the dishes — your help would probably be appreciated and apart from that, it's good manners to offer, even if your offer's rejected.

But above all, don't worry. After all, you've only been out with Les a few times, so it's not as though his mum is viewing a prospective daughter-in-law, so she shouldn't be too critical.

Enjoy yourself—and don't forget to take his mum a bunch of flowers or a box of chocs — and remember to thank her for a lovely meal!

Her Gift To Me Was Cheap And Nasty

DEAR CATHY & CLAIRE—I gave my friend a lovely present for her birthday last month, but when it was my birthday last week, she just gave me a cheap little brooch.

I felt really insulted that she could give me something as rubbishy as this and I told her exactly what I thought of it When I'd finished, she burst into tears and ran off, and now she won't even speak to me.

We're not surprised! The way you behaved was absolutely inexcusable and you should apologise to your friend as soon as possible.

Obviously she did not intend to "insult" you, it seems more likely that she just didn't have a lot of money to spend, and it's just unfortunate her taste differs from yours. After all, she didn't forget altogether—and it is the thought that counts.

So stop being so selfish and horrible and try to make up with her again—that is if she'll have anything to do with you! And in future don't be so mean and thoughtless.

I'm Terrified Of My Future

DEAR CATHY & CLAIRE — I'm really beginning to get worried about myself. You see, I really believe in horoscopes and things like that and it's starting to worry me. I always do what they tell me to do and they've often worked out.

I even went to a fortune teller last week and she told me a lot about myself. Well, one of the things she told me concerns my boyfriend. She said that the big romance of my life would fade away to nothing. I'm so scared now because I really love my boyfriend. I'm too scared to tell him about my fears in case it puts ideas into his head but I don't know what to do. I'm sure it's going to come true. What can I do to stop it happening?

You really must stop taking horoscopes so seriously. It's very unlikely they have definite bearing on your life and it could be quite harmful if you believe in them completely as you do.

Everyone reads them for a laugh but when you start to believe something that some fortune teller has told you — it's time to take things a lot less seriously.

How could she possibly foretell that you and your boyfriend are going to split up? She can't! So please try to remember that before you get yourself into a state.

We're not saying that he won't finish with you, but if he does, it's hardly likely to be because of what someone foretold. We're sure he'd have to have a much better reason than that.

You don't have to stop reading your horoscope — after all, they can be a good laugh, but never take them so seriously that they begin to affect your life — that can only lead to unhappiness.

My Best Friend Is
A Boring Bookworm

DEAR CATHY & CLAIRE — My problem is my best friend, Gail. Every time she comes round to my house, she finds the nearest magazine or paper which happens to be lying around and becomes completely engrossed for the rest of the evening!

I'm then ignored by her until it's time for her to leave.

I've tried telling her that she's rotten company, but she just laughs and takes no notice.

Help!

She's obviously pretty rude, but you don't need us to tell you that!

Short of hiding all the reading material in the house before her visits there's no real cure! She's probably just a compulsive bookworm!

Offer to lend her the magazines to take home and read afterwards, or try to arrange something specific to occupy you both for these evenings.

Having a sewing session, swop records or posters or even invite another friend round too.

She wouldn't bury her nose in a book then, as she'd probably be afraid of missing out on something!

I'm Bad At Games

DEAR CATHY & CLAIRE — Please can you help me get over the problem of P.E.? I absolutely hate it. I'm no good at netball, gym or hockey, and I'm beginning to get really worried about it. I do try, but that's beside the point. I just feel I'll never be able to do well.

My friends all take it as a joke, which I suppose is a good thing, but I'd still like some help.

So the only sort of physical exercise muddy fields, pitches and gymnasiums inspires you to is running until you've got out of sight of them! Why should that bother you so much? If you *accepted* that, instead of feeling you ought to change your attitude and your capabilities, and take it all as a joke like your friends do, you'll be on the right tracks! (Sorry!)

Honestly, though, we don't think you'll solve anything by trying to go against your nature and become the Sportswoman of the Year. The only thing you can try to change is the basic reason that makes you want to change yourself — and that, we'd make a pretty good guess, is because you want to join in and be one of the crowd.

O K, the team spirit creates a great "community" feeling, and common interests like games can give you a lot of inspiration and a sense of identity. But you can't achieve that by not being you, and if you laugh at yourself with the others, you'll find you're accepted anyway. Then if you still long for that sense of belonging to a crowd, why not get in with a group of people who are doing something you *do* enjoy?

Should I Go Out With Him?

DEAR CATHY & CLAIRE — I'm 13 years old, and I live near a gypsy site. There's a boy called Peter who lives on the site, and he keeps asking me out, but every time I make a feeble excuse not to go.

He's very good looking but I'm rather scared of him as the people he goes round with are rather wild.

Please try to advise me about whether I should go out with him or not.

It's all very well him being great-looking, but honestly, if you're in the least bit worried about him, better leave things as they are.

You feel you have to make excuses, right? That means you don't feel quite happy in yourself about taking the relationship further, so, honestly, we'd advise you not to.

When you meet somebody who's the right type for you, you won't have reservations about saying "yes" when he asks you out. So stop being feeble about your excuses, be definite and start going other places to meet other boys!

They Refuse To Get A Phone

DEAR CATHY & CLAIRE — I've just had the biggest row ever with my parents. It all started when my friend's parents installed a phone in their home. Now she's on at me to get my parents to have one but they won't hear of it. They won't even listen to me — Dad says he can't afford one and that's that.

Look love, face the fact will you? Your parents have told you they can't afford to have a telephone. They're completely honest about it, and as you aren't earning yet, it's pointless complaining. They're doing their best for you, and if their finances don't run into luxuries, then it's just too bad.

Explain to your friend that at the moment your parents can't afford one. If she's a friend at all she'll understand and won't put her foot in it again, and you can stop badgering your poor parents! OK?

All She Does Is Moan

DEAR CATHY & CLAIRE — Jenny, Mary and me always went around together, then Mary started going off with Pauline, and sometimes with some other people.

Jenny still goes around with me and we do the same sort of things we used to, but she's always moaning that it's not so much fun as when Mary was there.

I'm really fed up of hearing her moan, because at least I'm still there and you'd think she'd be grateful for that. I'm beginning to think that she's only friends with me because Mary has gone and she's got no choice.

We don't think you should pay too much attention to Jenny. Just think if you'd been the one to go, Jenny would be moaning on at Mary about how much better things were when you were there!

And we don't think Jenny goes out with you because she has no one else. She obviously thinks of you as a close friend — someone to share the nice times and listen to her moans. But it might be a good idea for both of you to expand your social lives by making a few more friends, thus not having to rely on each other for company quite so much.

Why Does She Get More Boyfriends Than Me?

DEAR CATHY & CLAIRE — My friend Alison is small and fairly plump, and yet she gets loads of boyfriends, but although I'm slim and fairly pretty, I've never had a boyfriend in my life.

When we go to the youth club, Alison usually wears the same shabby things but I get lots of new, trendy clothes so I look pretty good. The trouble is that Alison often gets walked home and asked for dates, but the boys only ever dance with me a couple of times and that's it — I just don't understand it.

How can I get a boyfriend?

With an attitude like yours, we're not surprised that you don't have any boyfriends!

Look, love, it's no good treating boys like possessions such as new clothes etc. You can't just go through life saying " I want " and expect to have it handed to you on a plate.

You obviously think that the best way to get a boyfriend is to look good which is true up to a point, but you've got to be a nice, interesting person, too, or the boy will soon get tired of you. Try paying a bit more attention to the boy and stop worrying so much about your looks.

Alison is probably a nice, fun-loving person and very easy to get along with which is why the boys like her, so try to be a bit more like her and stop feeling so superior!

Her Childish Games Have Gone Too Far

DEAR CATHY & CLAIRE – My friend really fancies this boy who lives nearby. She follows him everywhere and tells his friends that she likes him. In general making it dead obvious that she'd love to go out with him.

All this time I've played along with her games. But it was the last straw when she phoned his house and then put down the receiver when she heard him speak.

She's so childish that it's incredible!

Look, you're this girl's friend, but you still let her practise, and even participate yourself, in this stupid behaviour.

Surely you could tell her that she'll never succeed in acquiring a fella this way.

All she'll gain is the reputation for making a fool of herself. And it's time you both realised that!

How Will I Cope At The Airport?

DEAR CATHY & CLAIRE — I'm going to Canada soon for a three-week holiday. I'll be staying with my pen-pal and her family, and I'm really looking forward to it. There's just one thing that's worrying me a bit. I've never been inside an airport, and don't even know what it looks like, apart from what I've seen on telly. I'm travelling on my own and I'm sure I'll end up on the wrong plane or something!

Don't worry, love, your chance of boarding the wrong plane is virtually a thousand to one chance — mainly because the place is crawling with ground staff ready to help the uninitiated into the fine art of jet-setting!

It is a terrifying prospect, though, if you've never travelled alone, and don't have a clue what to expect, so we'll give you a rough idea of what it's all about.

Most important thing to do is keep your ears pinned well back to hear your flight number being announced over the tannoy. You'll already have a note on your air ticket of your plane's time of arrival and departure, so make a mental note of this, while you sit and watch the planes go by. In the main area of the airport, you'll find a huge notice board and digital clock, which you can't fail to miss. This will register the times of the planes arriving in the airport at the exact moment, and will also give a time of boarding the plane.

Congratulate yourself on being so independent and stay calm! If you start to panic, however, grab a ground stewardess and she'll be only too pleased to set you right. It's part of her job after all.

Happy holiday!

My New Shoes Are An Embarrassment

DEAR CATHY & CLAIRE — Dad decided that it was time I had some nice, "sensible" shoes, so he took me into town to buy a pair.

It was then that we discovered how much our tastes differ.

After trudging around for hours, we ended up in an expensive shop which stocked many styles — all of them hideous.

I eventually came out with a pair of extremely flat "flatties" which I swore I would never wear. They're a horrible mustard coloured suede with an enormous buckle on the front — and they really look out of place with my clothes.

Now my other shoes have worn out, so I've got to wear them because Dad says he can't afford to buy me another pair as they cost £8.50.

Please help me before my friends begin to think I've gone mad, because now I've got to wear them for school; uniform and all.

If you really hated the shoes, why did you let your dad waste his money on them? You could have said they hurt your feet, and then maybe your dad would have compromised and got you a pair that you both liked.

We don't suppose that they look too bad with school uniform, because, if you think about it sensibly, nothing can make school uniform look any worse!

Seriously though, love, we reckon you'll just have to hope that they're not the long-lasting type that are guaranteed not to wear out for at least five years.

And don't let your dad waste his money the next time — there are plenty of fashionable "sensible" shoes around!

I Lied About My Age

DEAR CATHY & CLAIRE — I've been going out with Gary for nearly two months and he still doesn't know I'm only sixteen. He's twenty three and I told him I was nineteen. You see, I met him at this very posh disco and he's very mature and sophisticated. I don't see him very often — so he hasn't found out that I'm still at school.

Well, I'm beginning to find this a terrible strain — pretending to be what I'm not. I don't want to lose him, though, so what do you think I should do?

You must tell Gary the truth immediately and tell him how old you are. This is really the only thing you can do. He's bound to be a bit angry because you lied to him and he may even think the age gap is too great. After all, he is seven years older than you — he might not like the idea of going out with a school girl.

He may, of course, not be worried about the age difference. If this is the case, you must also tell your parents how old Gary is and make sure that they have no objections. There's no point in deceiving them either. They might not be too happy about this so don't be too disappointed if they refuse to let you go out with Gary.

If neither Gary nor your parents have any objections about the age difference, well, fine.

But you really can't carry on your deceit any longer. You wouldn't be happy with someone you had to keep lying to, would you . . .?

He Won't Stop Calling Me

DEAR CATHY & CLAIRE, When Graham asked me to go out with him, I wasn't very keen, but as I wasn't doing anything else that night I agreed to go. And I've honestly never been so bored in all my life!

The trouble is, he keeps phoning me up and asking me out, and I don't want to go. At first, I was very polite, but now he's really getting on my nerves. I keep making up excuses and I've even tried putting the phone down when he's speaking but he won't take the hint. I don't want to have to be rude and tell him to get lost, but it looks as though I'll have to.

It sounds as though this boy is either crazy about you, or just plain dim. Either way, he's certainly persistent.

He will get fed up eventually, love, but until then, you'll just have to grin and bear it.

And anyway, doesn't it boost your ego a little bit to have someone pursuing you like this?

My Best Friend Is The Class Thief

DEAR CATHY & CLAIRE — My best friend isn't very well off and is always complaining about it. She's forever borrowing my clothes and large sums of money which she never repays. The worst of it is that recently considerable amounts of money have been missing from members of our form and although she confessed the thefts to me in confidence, to my horror, she continued to steal.

After one girl had money stolen, Laura later offered me half the money. Of course, I refused, but I would like to know the best possible way to tell her to stop thieving before she gets herself into real trouble.

Nobody suspects Laura — in fact another girl is being blamed. I just can't tell her mother — she's a widow and I know she'd be heartbroken. Help!

You'll *have* to have a straight talk with Laura now — before she ends up in a police court!

Tell her how selfish and mean her behaviour is — ask her how she would feel if her mother were informed. A hint in this direction should be sufficient to scare her into sense.

If not, then you must tell the story to a teacher or to your own mother. Perhaps they'll make her realise.

As far as the cash problem is concerned, suggest a Saturday job.

98

Will The Police Tell My Parents?

DEAR CATHY & CLAIRE — Last week I was having a drink with some friends when two policemen came into the pub. They guessed I was only 16 and took my name and address. They told me there would be someone along later in the week to see my parents.

It was only my first time, but I'm scared to tell my parents I'm in trouble. Do you think there's any chance they might forget about it, as it only happened once?

By the time you read this letter, love, you'll have found out the hard way they certainly WON'T forget it.

Under-age drinking is a rising social problem in Britain and if anyone is caught breaking the law, whether it's their first time or not, the consequences are the same; a court appearance, a possible fine, and a stern warning not to appear in court ever again. So it just isn't worth it and can lead to trouble in more ways than one.

I Need To Know How To Kiss

DEAR CATHY & CLAIRE — I'm very depressed. I go to parties and discos and sometimes meet boys, but the trouble comes when they ask for a goodnight kiss. That's the whole problem. I know it sounds daft, but I don't know how to kiss a boy. Please help!

What do you want us to say? Number one, put your lips into such and such a shape, number two, place hands round boy's shoulders . . . well, we aren't, because there just aren't sets of rules for it!

It might worry you when you think about it — so, don't think! Kissing someone's not really something that's expected of you, as part and parcel of going out together — at least, it shouldn't be.

If and when you want to kiss someone, you will, and it'll be natural and enjoyable even if it's shy and hesitant as it probably will be, at first! So forget all about hows and whys. When it feels the right thing to do — you'll do it!

True Love Is Making Me Miserable

DEAR CATHY & CLAIRE — Please, please try to help me. I'm in love with Alan Williams of the Rubettes. I know you'll say that it's a crush, but honestly, it's real love.

I cry about him every night and I listen to their records all the time. Don't tell me to forget him — I know I never will.

What can I do about this? — It's ruining my life.

We know you'll find this difficult to believe, but what you feel isn't love but infatuation or physical attraction. You can't possibly love a person you don't know.

This is really just a passing phase — you will get over him soon. When you have a real live boyfriend you really care about, you'll find this crush fading to the back of your mind.

In the meantime, don't let your life be ruled by dreams which can never come to anything. Develop new interests and get out and about with your friends. And, above all, don't worry. In no time at all you'll be wondering what on earth you *were* worrying about.

We won't tell you to forget him but try to like him as a musician and for what he is — someone you can respect and admire, but not someone to fall in love with.

My Identical Twin Pretended To Be Me

DEAR CATHY & CLAIRE — My sister and I are identical twins and we've always got on really well, until recently. The trouble started because I had a boyfriend and Julie didn't. She kept asking me why he'd chosen me, and not her, because we're both so alike. I couldn't think of an answer, so I just shrugged and said I was lucky.

Then, one night Jeff said something which I didn't understand and when I looked puzzled he said, "You agreed last night."

"But I haven't seen you for two days," I told him.

It was his turn to look puzzled and he said, "But we went out for a coffee last night when I called for you."

I'd been out to a friend's the night before, and I realised what must have happened. Julie had pretended to be me and had gone out with him. As soon as I got home I tackled her about it and she admitted that she'd been out with him several times. She was very apologetic and promised that it would never happen again, but Jeff has decided that he likes us both and wants to continue to take the two of us out.

I just don't see why I should share him — he is MY boy friend, but Julie thinks it's a great idea.

We think that it's time you had a good talk with Julie and told her that it's time she left Jeff alone.

The whole mix-up was her fault to begin with, so she is the one who should try to rectify the situation. If she has any intention of putting things right, she should apologise to Jeff — after all, she did make a bit of a fool of him — and leave the field clear for you again.

Have you given any thought to how much Jeff cares about you? Even if you are identical twins, we reckon he must be pretty gullible to have been taken in. Or maybe he realised what was going on, but didn't want it to change.

Think about it, love, it's possible that it wasn't ALL Julie's fault even though she was pretty underhanded and sneaky!

She's Making
A Fool Of Herself

DEAR CATHY & CLAIRE — Jan is in our class at school and she's managed to convince herself that a boy she thinks she's in love with really fancies her. Everyone else in the class knows that Dave can't stand the sight of her.

In fact, he likes Jan's best friend Pat. But Jan is convinced that he's only friendly with Pat so that he can be near to her.

We don't want to stand by and let her be hurt, but what can we do? Should we warn her now or just let her find out for herself?

Poor Jan, we really feel sorry for her. It's clear that she's going to get hurt whatever happens.

If you try to tell her the truth, there's a pretty good chance that she won't believe you — she seems to be rather good at kidding herself And even if she's aware that she's only deceiving herself, we think she might resent you ruining all her dreams; at least at the moment, she can still hope.

Sooner or later she's bound to discover the truth, so make sure that you're around to help her get over him.

He Doesn't Trust Me Behind The Wheel

DEAR CATHY & CLAIRE — My boyfriend gave me one driving lesson recently but I drove the car straight into a ditch.

And since then he's refused to teach me again. He says I only confirmed his belief that women make useless drivers.

Well, prove to him that they're not — by passing the driving test!

If you want to learn how to drive without any rows or arguments, go to a driving school. They won't lose patience with you like he has.

Of course it'll be expensive, but we reckon that the pleasure in saying you've passed, makes it well worth it.

My Trendy Gear Ruined Everything

DEAR CATHY & CLAIRE — All the spending money I get from my mum goes on clothes. I always dress in the latest fashion and enjoy people looking at me. My boyfriend is a trendy guy, too, or so I thought.

Anyway I arrived for a date, dressed in my latest gear, which he hadn't seen — and he wouldn't take me out! He said he was embarrassed to be seen with me. We had a blazing row and he walked out on me. I want him back but what can I do?

Well, as we see it, you've got a choice. Either you keep your trendy gear and lose your boyfriend, or you dress a little more conventionally and try and get your boyfriend back. If you want him back, that is.

Seems to us that he acted a little bit childishly, but then, it depends on what you were wearing, we suppose. I mean, if you turned up in multi-coloured socks, red jeans rolled up to the knee, sparkly green platforms and shocking pink bomber jacket, we'd say he had a point! If, on the other hand, you were dressed trendily but neatly, we'd say he possibly over-reacted.

Only you know the truth of the matter love, and only you know if you want him back. If you do — then you'll just have to go round to his house and apologise and, if you go back with him, leave all your trendy gear at home. It'll be safer that way.

My Brother Is Being Mean To Me

DEAR CATHY & CLAIRE—My brother wanted to borrow my new Elton John album to take to his friend's party. Although I wasn't too keen on lending it to him, he went on about it so much that I eventually gave in, just to shut him up.

The party was weeks ago and he kept saying that he'd forgotten and left my LP at his friend's house—but last night he admitted that it had disappeared during the party and that he didn't know who had taken it.

I am really upset about this and think that he should buy me a new LP, but he says that it wasn't his fault and that he has no intention of replacing it. It's not as though he can't afford to replace it as he's bought himself a couple of new LP's in the past few weeks.

We definitely think that your brother should buy you a new LP; he borrowed it and it was his responsibility to look after it.

If he didn't have enough money to replace it, it wouldn't make him seem quite so bad—but as he's bought himself a couple of albums this makes his behaviour inexcusable.

As he refuses to replace it, the only thing that we can suggest is that you have a word with your parents and see if they can persuade your brother to change his mind.

In future, love, don't lend your records out for parties unless you'll be there to keep an eye on them and make sure that they're treated with care. Records are so easily damaged or mislaid that it's always risky to lend them to anyone, no matter how well you know them.

110

Why Should I Stop Smoking!

DEAR CATHY & CLAIRE — I'm 15 and I've been smoking for nearly three years. I don't know what all the fuss is about smoking, it doesn't seem to be doing me any harm and I don't really care what other people say anyway. People are always saying that I should give it up but I don't really want to.

I enjoy smoking and it makes me feel better when I'm with a crowd of people — it gives me confidence. The only trouble with smoking is that I spend nearly all my pocket money on cigarettes. This is a bit of a nuisance because my parents keep asking me where all my money has gone and I don't know what to say.

My parents don't know I smoke and I think they'd be pretty mad if they found out. They don't smoke and they think it's a dirty habit. I don't care though. I want to smoke and I'm going to — whatever anyone else says. All the older girls at the discos and parties I go to smoke so I don't see why I shouldn't.

I haven't noticed anything wrong with my health since I've started smoking but people say it could affect me. You don't think any harm will come to me — do you?

Yes, we most definitely do! Smoking is unsociable; it ruins your sense of smell and taste. More important it affects your health — your breathing for instance: you will be more prone to chest and bronchial illness. There is also a definite link with lung cancer.

You obviously do have a problem here or else you wouldn't have bothered to write to us — you do feel guilty about the fact that you smoke, don't you? Even though you say you don't want to give up . . .

The sentence which tells us the most about your problem is the one that starts "All the older girls . . ." it sounds as if one of your reasons for smoking is to try to be "grown-up." This is a really stupid idea. Smoking won't make you look grown-up, you know — it usually makes you look stupid . . . and it won't impress anyone. You also say that smoking gives you confidence — you would be far better to feel confident in other ways — to know you look good and things like that.

We think you do want to stop and if you could manage this, it would be far more reason to be proud of yourself. This will be difficult, we know, but far better to stop now than to wait till you're older — the habit will be far more difficult to break then . . .

The best way to stop smoking is to keep occupied. Don't leave yourself with nothing better to do than smoke and don't leave yourself with no cigarettes at all. Whenever you feel the urge to have a cigarette, say to yourself — "I'll have one in half an hour" and when the half hour is up say the same thing again until you are absolutely desperate. In this way you will eventually lose the need for a cigarette. All you need is a little willpower.

We're not being goody-goody by trying to make you give up cigarettes. There's nothing smart about smoking and you must realise that it's dangerous to your health.

Please give up this habit — you can do it if you really want to . . .